MY EARTH, MY HOME

A Kid's Book About Why Protecting Our Planet Matters

Written by
Yolanda Kondonassis

Illustrated by
Joan Brush

Better World Kids Books
New York

Sky Pony Press
New York

*For my Amanda, who inspires me in ways I never could have imagined;
for my Dad, who has been there for me every step of the way; and to
the memory of Joan Scarangello, my dear friend and cheerleader.*
—YK

Sky Pony Press books may be purchased in bulk at special discounts for sales promotion,
corporate gifts, fund-raising, or educational purposes. Special editions can also be created to
specifications. For details, contact the Special Sales Department, Sky Pony Press, 307 West
36th Street, 11th Floor, New York, NY 10018 or info@skyhorsepublishing.com.

Sky Pony® is a registered trademark of Skyhorse Publishing, Inc.®, a Delaware corporation.

Visit our website at www.skyponypress.com.

Manufactured in China, 2021
This product conforms to CPSIA 2008

10 9 8 7 6 5 4 3 2 1

Library of Congress Cataloging-in-Publication Data is available on file.

Print ISBN: 978-1-5107-6925-0
Ebook ISBN: 978-1-5107-7018-8

Cover design by Brian Peterson and David Ter-Avanesyan
Cover illustration by Joan Brush

Dear Reader,

If you have chosen this book, I am pretty sure you are interested in protecting our Earth and learning about all the ways that we can help.

I am both a mom and a former kid. We grown-ups have a big responsibility to clean up our environment and make a plan for the future, but I also know that adults often need lots of help from kids and this messy planet thing is a BIG job.

Making good choices for our Earth is like caring for our homes and our bodies. Even though it may be easier to pretend it's not a big deal, talking and learning about how we can care for our environment right now will make a better future for all of us.

I hope this book helps you understand why it's so important to love and protect our Earth. It's the only home we have and we can all make a difference!

—*Yolanda Kondonassis*

Did you know that our Earth is round?

4

OF course you did!

Do you know what happens
when your home is a round planet?

It means that if you were to ride a bike
in a straight line for a VERY, VERY, VERY,
VERY, VERY long time, you would end up...

What if your house was **round?**
What if your round house got messy?

What if you didn't feel like cleaning up that mess
in your round house and you pushed it away
so you wouldn't have to look at it?
Where would that mess end up?

Earth is a lot like a round house, only MUCH, MUCH, MUCH BIGGER!

Our Earth has gotten messy. What should we do?

Clean it up!

REDUCE
REUSE
RECYCLE

When we face a new
challenge, it helps to know
as much as we can
about the problem
so we can fix it.

What makes our Earth messy?

Cars, trucks, and factories make pollution,
a mixture of dirty gases and liquids that goes out into
the air and into our rivers, lakes, and oceans.

What if we just try not to live next to a highway or a factory?

Would that keep pollution away from us?

13

Pollution goes up into the sky and forms a blanket of gas that holds heat within Earth's atmosphere.

That makes our whole Earth warmer and leads to...

problems like...

melting polar ice caps...

...and extreme
weather patterns.

Scientists call
this warming of our
Earth's temperature

CLIMATE CHANGE.

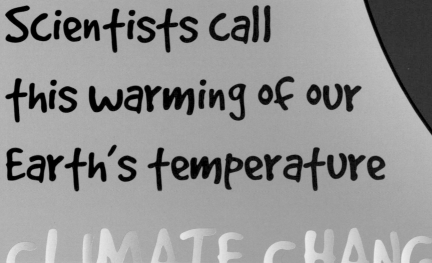

Pollution also comes back down to Earth as rain, and factories sometimes release waste into our rivers, lakes, and oceans.

This affects not only our water, but our plants and animals as well.

What happens when

we flip on a light,

watch TV,

use the washing machine,

or turn on a computer?

# of course not!

That cord we plug into the wall
connects to a big supply source
that provides energy for millions of people.

It's great to have
the energy we need,
but creating most kinds of
energy makes pollution and
uses up lots of natural resources.

That's why it's important to use only the energy we really need and think of ways to use even less.

What happens when
we crumple up
a plastic juice bottle
and
throw it away?

Or wad up
a piece of paper
and toss it into
the garbage can?

Does our trash just disappear into thin air poof! and get replaced by fresh new things?

# of course not!

Trash is either burned or dumped into gigantic holes in the ground called landfills.

Throwing less stuff away and recycling our trash are two big ways we can help protect our Earth.

In fact, recycling is a bit like real-life magic!

Recycled paper is made into books, magazines, folders, boxes, bags, tissues, paper towels, and of course, new paper.

Recycled aluminum cans are turned into new cans, foil, construction materials, and even car parts.

Recycled plastic bottles can become all sorts of things like carpet, clothing, picnic tables, sleeping bags, and flower pots.

Used glass can be recycled into new glass over and over again because it never loses its strength!

What could you recycle today?

When we reduce, reuse, and recycle,
fewer trees are chopped down
and that's good for our Earth.

Plus, we need our trees to eat up pollution
and help keep our air clean.

Did you know trees can do that?

Earth's forests are also home to many important animals and plants that help keep our world in balance.

Of course not!

But we need a plan and we all need to help.

MESSY PLANET ACTION PLAN
How many things on the following list can you do?

1. RECYCLE!

Talk with your parents about organizing your trash and help your family get into the habit of recycling paper, cardboard, plastic bottles, cans, aluminum foil, and clear glass bottles. Learn about your community's recycling system and do your part!

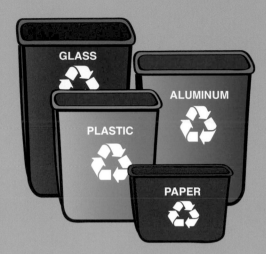

2. TURN OFF LIGHTS AND EQUIPMENT.

You can save lots of energy just by making sure to turn things off when you don't need them. Don't forget to unplug battery chargers—they use energy even when they aren't plugged into your devices!

3. DON'T DRIVE IF YOU CAN WALK OR CARPOOL INSTEAD.

Cars create tons of pollution that makes the air dirty. Walking is good for you and carpooling is a lot more fun than driving alone!

4. ASK YOUR PARENTS TO REPLACE BURNED-OUT LIGHT BULBS WITH NEW ENERGY-SAVING, LOW-WATTAGE BULBS.

Energy-saving light bulbs are now available just about everywhere. They last way longer than the old ones and use far less energy.

5. PLANT A TREE.

Trees eat up bad gases and help keep our air clean.

6. RECYCLE YOUR SHOPPING BAGS.

A huge amount of paper and plastic is wasted on shopping bags that are used only once. Save old ones and take them to the store when you shop, or buy a few sturdy bags that you always use for shopping.

7. USE LESS WATER.

Water is a precious resource and it takes energy to create clean water for drinking and bathing. Try taking shorter showers or turn off the faucet while you brush your teeth.

8. SHARE THIS LIST WITH A FRIEND.

EVERYONE CAN MAKE A DIFFERENCE!

OUR HOUSE IS ROUND

Our house is round, we know it's true,
like grass is green and the ocean is blue.
Air, land, and water fit like a glove
on this planet called Earth that we know and love.

But our Earth is sick, coughing and wheezing
like you with a cold, red-nosed and sneezing.
Our globe needs a break from the dirt in the air,
the junk in the water, and trash everywhere.

To start, we must use less and try to save more,
and care for this planet that we adore.
Recycle, don't waste, and tell all your friends
we must save our home—the job never ends.

It's time that we help and work together
to fix what's wrong and make things better.
We love where we live and it's certainly true,
our house is round and we know what to do.

WE CAN CLEAN UP
OUR PLANET TOGETHER!

About the Author

Yolanda Kondonassis is founder and director of Earth at Heart®, a nonprofit organization devoted to increasing earth awareness through the arts. Passionate about writing, earth conservation, and music, she is a multiple GRAMMY-nominated classical harpist with a love for kids and the desire to share both the power of knowledge and the inspiration for change. She is on the faculties of Oberlin College and the Cleveland Institute of Music.

About the Illustrator

Joan Brush is a fashion designer and illustrator with a background in children's literature and design. She received her BFA from the Rhode Island School of Design and launched a successful career as a sportswear designer shortly thereafter.